poems for
the Road

poems for the Road

IVIICAELA IVIEAD

ARTIVISTIC PRESS
New York

IVI
PRESS

116 West 23rd Street, 5th Floor
New York, NY
10011

First ARTIVISTIC Press paperback edition November 2019

ARTIVISTIC Press can bring authors to your live event. For more
information or to book an event, contact *events@artivisticpress.com* or visit
our website at www.artivisticpress.com/events.

BISAC: POETRY / Subjects & Themes / Nature | SELF-HELP / Personal
Growth / General | BODY, MIND & SPIRIT / Inspiration & Personal Growth.

LCCN 2019917588 | ISBN 9780578227146

Cover design by Micaela Mead

10 9 8 7 6 5 4 3 2 1

FOR THE WANDERERS

CONTENTS

PORTRAIT OF A GIRL

she always stood in one place. never moving.
never growing. waiting. waiting for the wind
to pick her up like a dandelion seed and carry her
far away. she dreamt of the future without imagining
it might one day become a reality. her reality.
this is the story of a girl who dreamt
with her eyes and mind closed. heart wide open
and vulnerable, but oh so scared of being scarred.
a girl who avoided the shadows without realizing
they reside inside her. she hid from the unknown
basking in the light of the familiar,
eventually utterly exhausted,
because two years is a long time.

A JAR OF STARS AND WISHES

I have a jar of stars

paper slips
filled and marked
by a child's dreams
untouched by dust
encased by glass

this jar once held smooth wax
of divine scent
heaven sent
a lovely lemon curd
thick enough to spread on toast
savoring of buttery sweetness
found pleasant on the tongue
heavy
heavenly
or heaven's scent
either way, delicious
yet tinged with a slight sharpness
the unmistakably tangy taste of lemon
in a jar

a jar of folded paper shreds
intricately and carefully designed

configured into stars
colorful and eye-catching
crafty
and unique

sometimes
I imagine that each of these stars is a wish
a secret
meticulously collected
from the hearts and minds of children
everywhere

what would I see
etched into the paper
if I dared to reach in
and pluck out a star?

if it were that I opened one
patiently unfolding every pressed crease
to read the words underneath
what might the letters reveal to me?

what might it say
if I leaned in close
and listened?

would it whisper to me

the secrets of a troubled mind
or a naïve heart?

or
perhaps
would that paper star
say nothing at all?

the likeness of an abandoned hope
a long forgotten dream
a lost reality
that would never be
left on the reckless shores of adulthood
swallowing the fantasies of a child
maybe, then, if this is the case
those wishes are best left
undisturbed
on display
for one and all
to see and admire
or to wonder at
as I have today
but never to know or discern

still, sometimes, I gaze at the paper stars
imagining
what it would be like

to choose
to unscrew the lid
held fast by time and disuse
to pour out all the tiny paper stars
in a cascade of dreams
and I think
if I did
maybe, just faintly
the jar might still smell
lingeringly
like lemons

IN SPIRES

made of ages
the richest rock
stretches on toward the heavens
all I've known
mountains stand
God's great architecture

but we have different gods here

beacons of glass
in spires aspiring to heaven
a winding staircase
with not so many steps
they urge you not to trip
over your feet
going up

STOLEN

go ahead and place a scarecrow
to guard your precious gold
which you transplanted in our patina rainforests
transfigure your ivory to steel
or more ivory to steal
and kill all that's real
as we wait
watching you build an iron gate
you may call me jaded
but I'm still watching for a green flash or sunburst
along the horizon
as the icecap melts into a puddle

RISING TIDES

they say the world's your oyster
but what do they mean by that?
if the world's my oyster
then why the hell's its shell so cracked?
I wouldn't eat it
don't care about no pearls
they say the world's our oyster
but an oyster is our world

warming waters, rising tides
do we say who lives, declare who dies?
is there any sense behind our eyes?
or just more lies to hide behind?

they say things will get better
but I don't think that's true
I've seen the piles of garbage
and miles of floating bottles
left behind by me and you
don't like 'em
don't buy 'em
the cost's too high to justify them
so tell me
how can you?

seasons come and seasons go
but we keep coming up with reasons
to do the things we know
are killing us and will disrupt
the course of all we know

will we change, will we grow?
is this the legacy we choose?
I've seen firsthand the drastic impact
left behind by me and you

warming waters, rising tides
is there any sense behind our eyes?
do we say who lives, declare who dies?
how can we attempt to moralize more lies?

will we change, will we grow?
or will we see our sons and daughters buried
by the tide of all we leave behind?
this is what we stand to lose

they say things will get better
but they won't unless we choose
to change our ways
and start today…
which begins with the things we do

this starts
and ends
with me
and you

HIGH SOCIETY

ripples in the crowd
filter down like words upon deaf ears
do you ever scream when no one hears?
listen hard, but never carefully
hoping your inauthenticity will set you free
you look down your nose at me
does that make you happy?
I know you can't be.
a highlight reel might have mass appeal
but it isn't actually real
you've been blinded by the light
and now the high of the high life is all you see…
but flashing lights fade to obscurity

SURFACE VALUES

I love your mask
I love the way it hides your face
who are you?
I don't care, you're gorgeous
don't take it off
don't shatter the illusion
let's just make believe

I love your mask
I like the way you hide who you are
behind your own face
is it your face
when it no longer resembles
the truth
of who you are?

in any case
don't shatter the illusion
let's just make believe
this is our truth

if I toss some words in the air
I hope you don't catch them
after all, our words don't matter
so just let them fall

below
sticks and stones
ripple in waves
and leave their effect
on some hidden, lost, unknown or forgotten
cityscape
obscured beneath a placid exterior
an identity in ruins
a false façade
but my what a beautiful reflection
of you
even if it is a bit
blurry at the edges

APPEARANCES

caught up in appearances
we may never see
the spark that burns within
beneath the surface

BENEATH THE SURFACE

what is with the world?
does anyone have a clue what is going on?
what's going on?
does anyone have a clue?
it's nothing new, really…
not to me
and not for you
we're all just muddling through
trying to decide what to do
and coming up with nothing

empty bank accounts
love that runs out
or never starts
broken hearts…
we're all parts
pieces
not a single whole
and yet there are so many holes
in our lives
and our minds

our lies
our truths…
where do those reside?

inside? outside?
who's to decide?
what lies our scars hide
what scars our lies hide
what lies.
what lies beneath
the surface of all our uncertainty?

in our lives lie our truths
as for me
I fight to dream, to learn, to love, to hope
I'm striving to thrive
but barely staying afloat
I'm trying to be me
but I don't know how to be happy
I'm trying to be happy
but I don't really know how
to be
me

PLASTIC

ribbons of glass
like cuts along my arm
as I carry the weight of the world
in my hands
your stares
and the questions you ask
do me less harm
than the things we keep bottled up
but for now we're safe
inside a shell
of color and perplexity
it's all just as well
you can't reach me
manicured and mannequin-ed
encased in a sheet of ice
a modern harlequin
colored in shades of the night
the grin on my face
a plastered mask
in place of the feelings I hide
yet even in my private hell
I'm safe
though I'm a shell
this tide has displaced
I'm not plastic and fake

just too tired
to take another stab
at your pride
and it's all just as well
that you can't reach me
there is nothing of substance to say
and not much left of us anyway

TWENTY EIGHT

sometimes I worry I won't make it past 27
every time I hear the clock strike eleven
I'm already fearing fate
facing the pace of each day
like
woah
hold up
wait!

I just wanna make it
all the way to 28

I just wanna make it
all the way to 28
but sometimes I worry
I might not make it another day

I contemplate:
what if I don't wake?
game over and I'm gone
like a yawn
slipped past the lips of fate
could I miss greeting another day's dawn?
yeah, I worry
the last of my last day might fade away before long

so when I hear the clock strike eleven
I'm already fearing fate

I just wanna make it
all the way to 28

but sometimes I worry
I might not make it another day

live fast, die young
always seemed like a line in a song
but now it's a ride I might find myself on
and
damn
I worry I might see the flip-side before long

live fast, die young…
yeah, I try to stay strong
but sometimes that seems like the path
I might
find
myself
on

and it's hard to stay strong
when the upside is gone

so I worry
I might not see the night's shade lightened by dawn

man, it's hard to stay strong when your up slides
down
and right becomes wrong

when you're upside down
does right become wrong?

yeah, I wanna make it all the way to 28
but today I'm just trying to outlast 27
sometimes I worry
I won't make it past the gates of heaven
oh, I'm worried I might not see the shade of this
night brightened by dawn

if I die before I wake
I pray the Lord my soul to take
but for heaven's sake…
I hope heaven waits
early admittance through those pearly gates
is just one more afterparty
that I don't wanna make

DISAPPEAR

yeah I've got a million reasons to disappear
but I'm still here
and the dark is so heavy
I try to bide my time
but the night is so steady and it blinds me
sometimes
when it finds me
I hide
when I'm feeling unsteady and I just want to cry
I think what if I die
and then I think of all of the people and things I'd be
leaving behind
and it's like someone turned a light on to brighten
the night from inside
I've got a million reasons but I'm still here
because of the one reason that brought me here

GIVE UP

I thought that I was stronger
but I don't wanna live like this
thought I could keep on keeping on
but somewhere along the line
something changed
maybe I changed my mind
or something else just changed inside
either way, now I find
I don't wanna live like this any longer

I don't wanna live in a world
characterized by hatred, violence, and pain
where corruption and suffering play
a never ending refrain
so I fill my lungs with sadness
and let my chest expand
over and over in repetition
till it's more than I can stand

scattered shards amidst torn and tattered pages
slow depression moves in stages
it permeates and saturates
sunny days in cloying haze
but it's not over
until you give in, give up, roll over

under their command

no, I don't wanna live in this world
characterized by hatred, violence, and pain
where uninterrupted corruption and suffering
might always remain
but rewind
and sometimes you'll find
broken glass lets more light in

just rewind
and sometimes you'll find
broken glass lets more light in

A LITTLE LONGER

if I died today
would anyone say
I wish you had stayed a little longer?

I know they say the hits that you take
will somehow make you stronger
but I just feel they've made my way
take just a little longer

I can't help feeling that I did this wrong
like I lived my life
but it took too long

is that an advantage or a detriment?
maybe it's a message that was heaven-sent
or just some meaning left to reinvent
with fresh intent
maybe I can start again
if I can just hold on…

if I died today
would anyone say
I wish you had stayed a little longer?

I know they say the hits that you take
will somehow make you stronger...
and I truly feel they've made my way
in ways I can barely ponder

all my weary stumblings
and bleary, blind blunderings
have forged this path I wander

now I'm restarting from the end
with all the secrets in hand
and though my path is mine to trod
alone
I think of your soul as I wander along

I ache in my bones as I wander along
and
I wish you had stayed
a little longer

PUSH

you keep pushing me
in directions I don't wanna go
and you keep pressing me for perfection
but your inflection says you don't wanna know
if you're asking for perfection
then I think you should know

or else you should go
just go

sometimes it's so hard to draw the line

I'm craving peace
but at war with my thoughts
and this is all I've got

I have so many thoughts
about who I am and who I might be
at the back of my mind:
do you like me?
I don't wanna fight, but I hold a hurricane inside
its rain escapes from out my eyes

it's push and pull
but I just wanna let it go
I just wanna let go

if I let go
how far will I fall?
if I can't see at all
where is the ground down below
is it too far for you to throw me a rope?

you try to bring me back down to earth
but you don't realize
my soul is tethered to the skies

I hold the universe inside

BEATEN

you beat me down
but somehow need me now
huh
don't fool yourself
don't kid
you're still on the outside looking in
top tier, bottom shelf
upper echelon of your sphere of hell
so low that you still don't hear me
well
I'm on another level in another state of mind
go an extra round, an extra mile, or take another hit
on the ropes or with the ring, heroes never quit
like a one with six zeros after it
give it one million percent
and yet
still on the outside
looking in
repeating lines
I'm on a different page
and I won't give up
the word is love
and cheater's never win

UNREACHABLE

hello my love
my heart
I just wanted to let you know
that I need to leave
I'm gonna go
and I'm gonna be
unreachable
for a while
if you need me
I'll be off grid
unplugged
lost?
maybe
a little
because
I walked a mile in my shoes
and got lost in the maze of my mind
tangled in a blanket of blue haze
I don't know about you
but I find
the sharpest gaze sometimes holds the most pain
inside
I'm sorry
I need to leave
I'm going home

and I'm gonna be
unreachable
for a while
so if you need me
I'll be off grid
I won't get your call
but if you send a smoke signal
it might reach me
just before the whole forest goes up in flames
that's all

RUNNING

I'm running to get there
I'm running to escape
each step I fall back
is more than each step I take
the acid rain keeps falling
like tears upon my skin
as all the memories converge
which I've fought to hold
within
it's far too late to turn back, in fact it always was
too late, too late, too late
a hurting, violent buzz
the words within my skull, resounding as I look back:
running down an endless trail
a painful, plaguing track
at each sharp and twisted turn
I nearly lose
my breath
but I force myself to keep on
placing one more haunted step
plod, plod, plod
my feet slip thickly in the mud
oh God, oh God, oh God
I relive what I have done
and left undone

there is nothing here
for me
nothing left of me
at all
the pounding rain stings and bites my skin
and I wish that I could fall
but I remain upright, with demons at my heels
in the dim and fading light
I consider what it means to feel
I contemplate the way to heal
and my feet sound like a burdened drum
as I
run and run and run
looking on to that distant mountain
seeking on toward what's to come

MOUNTAIN TOWN

wild huckleberry lemonade is sweet
and bitter
on my tongue
tasting both of distant places and memories
songs familiar and unsung
monarchs swallow their tails in the shade
children play hopscotch
on a chalkboard of polished purple stone
a primrose path is the sparkling brick road
to the wild blue yonder
always leading me home

I found The Fountain of Youth
in a babbling brook
most would miss
on their way
and found myself wandering home

I found The Fountain of Youth
in a babbling brook
and took a stone for the road

WAVES

there is a lot of pain in you
I feel it
I hope you permit yourself to feel it too
allow it to fill you up
truly embrace the blue
let the waves
descend
purify your soul
wash you clean
lighten you
and make you new
dive into the sadness
vanish beneath the surface
let the waves
fill you with purpose
let the waves
pour salt in your wounds

BURDEN

before you get it off your chest
you must be sure

you must be sure
it will not become the other's burden to carry

that's hardly fair
is it?

SO RUN

so run
as fast as your legs can carry you
far and away
up mountain and hill
through valleys
and still
keep running
run
as fast as you can
between trees
across beaches
feel the sand roll
between your toes
until you feel your soul
reconnect to the earth

UNCHARTED TERRITORY

she turned the small, round objects slowly in the
palm of her hand. one, two, three, the mystery seeds
slipped from her fingers and fell to the earth like
pebbles or rainfall, sprouting a landscape of
uncharted territory. as the trees grew up around her,
she dug in her bag for the necessary tools. striking a
match, she held a burning map to light her way.

CHANGING THE NARRATIVE

changing the narrative
is this what you're scared of?
the only thing I've inherited
is the inability to dare to live
but I'm changing the narrative
working every day to disparage it
but hurting every day is disheartening
sometimes I find myself fighting this
other times I just want to give in
but I'm changing the narrative
and no one said this would be easy

PROOF

they say "stay in your lane"
"this is so lame"
or "this ain't your game"
but it's insane
because in doing so
they act
like
we're all one and the same

make no mistake
I'm so grateful to all my brothers and sisters
and all of the others
who went out and paved the way
so I can stand here today

because of them I have the chance to say
even though our stories change
and we give different things different names…
we're all at once all unique and the same

see
that's why I came
to do the things you proclaim you cannot do

to bring the bigger picture into view
for you
no, I'm not concerned
with a grand debut

I don't have to prove who I am
to prove who I am
and I don't have to prove who I am to you
who I am doesn't come after you
no better or worse, I ain't half of you

we all have worth and that's the truth

so just let me speak
don't get in my way
please let me preach what I came here to say
and maybe
if you listen
my words will blow you away

CURRENT

don't buy into "true"
are you really "free"?
I believe in two things:
compassion and creativity

don't buy into true
nothing's really free

in this new world order
creativity is currency

REGRETS

an education
they said
think of your education
just be practical
think of your future…

I am
I said

but no one listened

a mistake
they say
think of your education
you're not being practical
learn from our pasts

not my future
I say

they shake their heads

I see two paths:
yours and mine

intertwined
or separate?

can I do this?
you say I can't

do I listen
or do I take a stand?

these are my dreams
not yours
so let go
let me go

so let's go

amazing
they'll say
how did you do it?

I didn't listen
I'll say
I thought of my future
and I didn't
take no
for an answer

DEAR KID

dear kid,
you can be anything you want
when you grow up
we'll be here for you
and always show up
we all make it work somehow
so trust
and pray
and just
work hard
every day
but try not to dream too big, now…

GROW UP

when I was a child
they said "you can be whatever you want"
grow up to be a doctor
or a savior or an astronaut
but there's a forgotten caveat

it's the American Dream
but lucky Lady Liberty's lost her pristine sheen
we keep stacking cash
and obsess over the past
'cause nothing's what it seemed

say, back then
when we were ten
wish we could go back there again

I used to be wild
I said whatever I thought
grew up to be a fighter
so much braver than I thought
but there's a forgotten caveat

it's the American Scheme
'cause nothing's what we dreamed
so now we're all choking

holding in screams
the final exhale of our dying dreams

way back when
while we were ten
wish we could go back to then
but we can't go back again

WATCH ME

they say "you can't do this"
or "this is who you should be"
but I disagree
just watch me, you'll see
they say "you can't do this"
or "this is who you should be"
but I disagree
watch me
and then follow my lead

ODDS ARE

stupid, stupid, stupid
yeah, you might say I never learn
but the truth is
I'm learning while I'm earning
and the truth is
you could use this
but you might lose it
I hope you pay close enough attention
to go ahead and roll the dice
and play it right
pretty soon
it'll be your turn

DREAMCATCHER

when I take a step in a new direction
I fall back with every one
there's nothing left, I gain no traction
my mind decides there is no reason
but my heart and soul know
I'm far from done

gotta get up, get out
get out of this town
jump in the front or back
and roll the windows down
this new day is the only one

you're never gonna make it here
is what they always say
but it's just a phrase that I don't hear
I'll do it anyway

gotta get up, get out
get out of this town
jump in the front or back
and roll the windows down
when there's nothing more for you to show
but things you've never done
that's when you run, drive, fly on

to meet the sun
chasing down that disk of gold
until what you seek is what you become

SIX MINUTES

six minutes might not seem like a lot
but it's the difference
between life and death

you'll know this if you've ever played witness
to a baby drawing their first breath
or seen a loved one passing on

remember that
when time feels
insignificant

just start there
start
with six minutes

THE WRONG PLACES

you're still looking for love
in all the wrong places
searching for souls in made-up faces
don't you know
bleeding hearts sometimes take a vacation

you keep seeking validation
in all the wrong places
fighting for breath in insignificant traces
instead of finding strength and endurance
in you

and you're searching for light
in all the wrong places
light is not found in a peaceful night
in truth
it's in the darkest places at the darkest times
to renew and repair and resist and remind

no, those aren't seeds that you plant in the ground
but these are seeds
you can plant
any time
true love and light grow to your own validation
and all of these things begin with your mind

WINDOWS

in the rickety, reckless, gritty mess
that we call the lonely ecstasy of life
you might find peace within the chaos
if you throw open the grimy windows of your mind

STAGES

I am a leaf collecting water in a rainstorm.
I am an upturned leaf, gathering dew in the night.
I am an overturned leaf, sloughing a deluge as it
runs in cool rivulets down my sides.
I am an upturned leaf, basking in the glow of the
sun, face gathering in the heat.
I am a leaf, still in the solitude of silence.
I tremble in a breeze.

SO IT GOES

the lowest lows
juxtapose
the highest highs
so you'll open your eyes
and realize
that sometimes
what you need
to revitalize your soul
or fill a hole
and help you grow
is rain from cloudy skies

OUT OF THE BLUE

leapfrog tradition
taking a taxi to the cliff's edge
trade in blue suede shoes for old leather boots
out of the blue
breathe in
a tropical and atypical breath of fresh air

SMOKE SIGNALS

once upon a time
I was aimless in a corn maze
a night owl
reading strokes of graphite
drawn from your muddy quarry
by genie lamp
tongue-tied, waffling for response
hoping for a smoke signal
but I let my feet wander
and stumbled over an ant hill or a gold mine
in the darkness
cracking glass crunched beneath
and my genius broke free
till the cornsilk wove itself around me
and the brittle stalks blazed
that cornfield burnt for days and days

MAGMA

we are all molten
we are fiercest at our weakest
heat-charged molecules of molecular potency
our fluidity is celebratory
our flexibility revelatory
and we will regenerate

BREAKING FREE

I'm not my mother or father
and I am not yesterday's son
I'm not broken
I'm a wide open highway with room to run

no, I am not my mother or father
and I am not yesterday's son

I'm not broken
I'm wide open
a spacious highway
with freshly painted lines
to be used as a guide
and plenty of room to run

TOWN & COUNTRY

I've been a town mouse and a country mouse
and lived in the city for a year or four
I love the glow of the lights
though sometimes they shine a little bright at night
they always make me feel much less alone
but I still ache for a feeling of home
at the same time
I pine for the unknown
so, perhaps at some point I'll decide
I'd like a house in the country more
you know, I've lived many lives
and thought them all nice enough
but someday I might find I've had quite enough
of the hustle and bustle which go with this flow
enough to give up this life
and go
a country mouse moved out
vacated the high rise or fancy townhouse
a town mouse gone native
moved
back to my roots
again returned to the countryside
a plant set to seed, an animal set loose
to be sure
I think I might like a quiet life a bit more

RECIPE FOR TRUE BLISS

the recipe for bliss
is as follows:
unfollow
unsubscribe
downsize
minimize your TO DO list
maximize joy
move more
give more
love more
DO LESS

this is the recipe for true bliss.

THERE'S STILL SOMETHING

there's a chill inside me that I can't control
it settles in my bones
and is threatening my soul
but after all this suffering
there's still something to be told
the future favors the living
like the journey favors the bold

I'D RATHER BE PRETTY

I'd rather be pretty than beautiful
pretty strong, pretty wise
pretty smart, pretty kind
to seek to spread love, hope, and warmth
as opposed to simply picking a side
yes, I'd rather be pretty than beautiful
pretty strong, pretty kind
pretty smart, pretty wise
to see through the lies which deceive so many eyes
and know the true beauty which all the world holds
inside

PORTRAIT OF A WOMAN

two years is a long time.
long enough for a seed to grow
or for a child to make her first unbalanced steps.
and then run. fall down. clumsy. that's me.
but I now know how to pick up pieces.
I learned to pick myself up and put the pieces of me
together as best I could. better. I used to dream,
but now my eyes and mind are wide open.
a go-getter. no longer dreaming of the day the
future
becomes reality, because my future IS my reality.
and I possess the power to make it what I will.
and I will. watch me.
but don't blink. you might miss me
as I slip among the shadows.
I am—they are. beautiful. dark, mysterious. whole,
complete.
complex. in the space of that time, I grew up,
and grew into the space I now occupy.
I fashioned my crown from vines plucked from
thorny, unstable ground.
go ahead and try to knock me down. I dare you.

POEMS FOR THE ROAD

it's a rocky one we're on, isn't it?
you're going to need some poems in your pocket
and maybe some rocks to kick
or maybe what you need
is some stones in your pocket
and some poetry to lift your spirit…
your soul is so weary
I hear it
but you're on a journey
and baby, I know you can bear it
but on the days that you can't
maybe we can share it?
I'm a stone's throw away
in the poems you hold

you may tear out a page
to carry them with you
ignite light in your soul
and brighten your view
and make the road feel like home
wherever you go
whatever your pace
fast or slow
I hope you get lost in the glory
of the steps that you're taking

revel in your story
it's all of your making
and I'll always be waiting in these pages, you know
I'm just a stone's throw away
in the poems that you hold
I hope you'll carry them with you
to lighten your load

ABOUT THE AUTHOR

MICAELA MEAD is an eco-warrior, artivist, and wordsmith who prefers the pronouns she, her, and hers. She is most chiefly motivated to provoke thought and facilitate conversation through innovation in a variety of artistic disciplines, and seeks to spread love and positivity with her work. In addition to *Poems for the Road*, her previous works include *ARTIVISTIC*, *Wisdom & Sh*t*, and a revealing collection of poems titled *Naked Truths*. She lives by the principles of sustainability, incurable idealism, and a healthy dose of magic. When she isn't writing or making art, she can most often be found watching squirrels or devouring vegan food in New York City.

ACKNOWLEDGMENTS

Truly, I have you to thank for this book. I know we're all on separate journeys and our individual struggles and triumphs are all our own. That said, I can and will in no way pretend I know what you have been through, are going through, or might go through in the future. All I know for certain is that I have experienced my own versions of pain and pure joy, and my heart aches for you in all aspects of your individual existence every second of every day. Because no matter how unique we might be as individuals, we are also part of a collective experience, and that shapes us in innumerable ways as well. I'd like to thank you for existing with me. I love you with every fiber of my being, and I am proud of every decision you make (whether mundane or masterful) to live your best life and show up as your best self every day. If no one has told you today, you are loved. If no one has told you today, you are worthy. If no one has told you today, YOU ARE ENOUGH. Thank you for existing and persisting. You make this world so much brighter.

xx

www.ingramcontent.com/pod-product-compliance
Lightning Source LLC
LaVergne TN
LVHW051427080426
835508LV00022B/3270